Let's Talk About

TEASING

By JOY WILT BERRY

Produced by Martin Kasen
Edited by Orly Kelly

Designed by Jill Losson

Copyright© 1982 by Joy Wilt Berry

First Printing, July 1982

Published by
PETER PAN INDUSTRIES
145 Komorn Street
Newark, NJ 07105
ISBN NO. 0-88149-010-5

Let's talk about TEASING.

When people annoy you or make fun
of you in playful ways, they are
TEASING you.

Has anyone ever teased you about the way you *look?*

Has anyone ever teased you about the way you *think* and *feel*?

Has anyone ever teased you about what you *say* or *do?*

Has anyone ever teased you about what you *like* and *don't like?*

Whenever someone teases you, you probably feel frustrated, embarrassed, and "put down."

When someone teases you, you may get upset and become angry.

People who tease often enjoy frustrating and embarrassing others.

They enjoy upsetting others.

Thus, you please the person who is teasing you when you become frustrated or upset.

If you want someone to stop teasing you, you must not become frustrated. You must not get embarrassed or become upset.

To make sure that you do not do these things, you must *ignore* the people who are teasing you. Do not pay attention to what they are saying.

If it is hard for you to ignore them, *walk away* from them. Do not stay around them while they are teasing you.

It is important to treat other people
the way you want to be treated.

If you do not like it when other people tease you,
you should not tease other people.

It is best not to talk about things that a person does not want anyone to talk about.
You should also not tell another person's secrets.

It is best not to say embarrassing things about another person in front of others.

It is best not to say anything to people that may hurt them.

A good rule to remember is —

*If you can't say something nice,
don't say anything at all.*

If you do this, you may be sure that
you will not hurt other people.

Teasing may hurt someone, so it is best not to do it.

A Note to Parents

Please let me help you! I have raised two children and worked with countless others. Believe me, I know what you are going through. For too long we parents have been made to feel that we alone are responsible for our children's successes or failures. This is an overwhelming and unfair burden. It is time for our children to assume some responsibility for their own lives. They can, if we will show them how and then give them a chance to do it.

This is where the <u>Let's Talk About</u> series comes in. Its purpose is—
- to help children to become aware of their behavior;
- to give children an understanding of why they do the things they do;
- to help children to see why their behavior may need to be changed;
- to tell children exactly what they can do to change their behavior.

The <u>Let's Talk About</u> series is EDUCATIONALLY, DEVELOPMENTALLY, and PSYCHOLOGICALLY sound. In addition to my being a parent, I am an educator and child developmentalist and have also worked extensively in the field of psychology. That is why I have made these principles the foundation of this series.

EDUCATIONALLY SPEAKING, children are capable of learning subject matter relevant to their lives and are eager to do so. The <u>Let's Talk About</u> series deals specifically with subjects that children experience almost every day of their lives.

DEVELOPMENTALLY SPEAKING, children have a right to grow and develop at their own pace. We, as parents, should not do anything to push or to inhibit them.

PSYCHOLOGICALLY SPEAKING, children will be healthy, productive people only if they understand themselves and are able to function in the world they live in.

The <u>Let's Talk About</u> series allows children to explore themselves openly and honestly. It also encourages them to express themselves in healthy, socially acceptable ways.

The <u>Let's Talk About</u> series is for children. It is natural for these children to be egocentric. That is why this series focuses on egocentricity. It helps children to understand their self-centeredness and how it affects them and others.

This understanding may not propel children into social responsibility, but it will provide them with the insights they need to move, on their own, from one stage to another with intelligence and sensitivity.

The <u>Let's Talk About</u> series will improve your parent-child relationships. If the relationship you have with your child is a normal one, you may be weary of lecturing to him or to her. If you are tired of talking, you may be sure that your child is tired of listening! Allow the <u>Let's Talk About</u> series to do the talking for you.

You probably know by now that your child often responds well to information that comes from an outside source. This series will give both you and your child a fresh new approach to working with tired old problems.

Before you know it, you and your child will be going in the same direction more of the time. This is because you will both be focusing on the same issues and functioning from the same premises.

Thank you for letting my work become a part of your lives.

Joy Berry